Our Experiment Goes to Outer Space

Penelope Santos

Rosen
Classroom
New York

Outer space is outside planet Earth.
There are many stars, planets, and
moons. Let's learn about it.

Space shuttles travel into outer space. A space launch is the start of the flight.

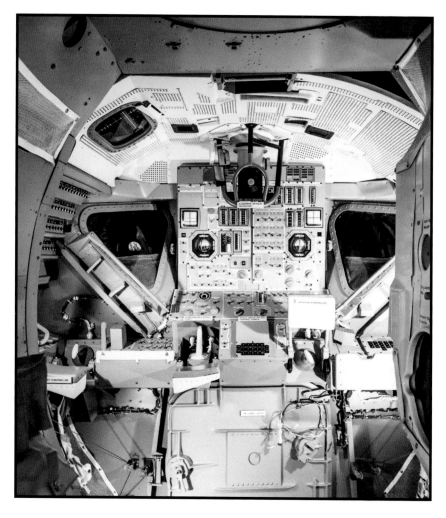

This is the inside of the shuttle. Our experiment will go in the shuttle. The shuttle has everything an astronaut would need in space.

Our experiment is a space rover. A space
rover is a robot that collects samples
from space.

A person that travels to outer space is an astronaut. Astronauts wear special suits to keep them safe. The suit allows astronauts to breathe in outer space.

There is no oxygen in space. Humans need oxygen to breathe. Helmets help astronauts breathe. Our experiment does not need oxygen.

There is very little gravity in space. Without much gravity, things float. This astronaut uses a safety tether so that he doesn't float away. Safety tethers help astronauts stay in place.

You can watch the shuttle with a telescope. A telescope helps you see into outer space.

No one knows how big space is. Shuttles travel farther and farther every day.

This space rover has traveled many miles. What kind of things do you think we will learn from it?

Glossary

experiment A test to discover something new.

launch To set something in motion.

space rover Machine made to travel across other planets.

telescope A tool used to see faraway distances.